The Surge

The Surge

An Overview of China's Rapidly Evolving Corporate Governance and Coming ESG Revolution

By Lyndsey Zhang

BoardEpoch Inc. (DBA: Boardroom&Beyond)
Greater Chicago Area
United States of America
www.boardroomandbeyond.com

ISBN 978-1-7368674-0-2
ISBN 978-1-7368674-1-9 (eBook)

Cover Design By Doudou Lv @ CENOZOIC

Printed in the United States of America

To my husband, Dong Jiang:
This journey won't be possible without your support and encouragement!

Contents

Part 3   The Evaluation: Measuring Corporate Social Responsibility (CSR) and ESG Practice in China

Part 4   The Future: New Challenges and Opportunities

Acknowledgements

This book would not be in print if not for the help of the following colleagues, mentors, friends and assistants:

While the seeds of the book were planted years ago, they did not grow until I had the chance to work with Professor Lourdes Casanova, Director and Senior Lecturer of Management at the Emerging Markets Institute at Cornell University. Professor Casanova and her colleague, Professor Anne Miroux, sharpened my writing, caused me to dive deeper into my research and expanded my understanding of this topic.

Bob Tricker (widely considered the "Father of Corporate Governance") and Gregg Li, co-authors of *Understanding Corporate Governance in China*, inspired and encouraged me every step along the way in my corporate governance research and writing. Having the opportunity to exchange ideas with these corporate governance experts gave me courage to pursue my own path. I am especially thankful for Dr. Li's contributions and support during the final editing of this book.

Many thanks to Boardroom&Beyond's professional team led by David Warren who did an excellent job editing and formatting the book.

Two of my colleagues who would like to remain anonymous contributed profound insights regarding Chinese companies' governance practices. Many other colleagues and friends not named here have been great sources of knowledge and wisdom during this journey.

In the end, the opinion expressed, and any errors in this book, remains my own.

Foreword

Corporate Governance (CG) has continued to evolve around the world, and in China, it has taken a life of its own since the onset of their Four Modernization that started in 1978. China has become one of the definitive modern playgrounds of evolving practices by 2021 and bears watching from practitioners and academics alike. Lyndsey has dared to push the understanding of ESG as it is being practiced in China. With her work here, and in so doing, she has made us all a little wiser and allowed us a peek into a different world of possibilities.

As in any good playground, there is bound to be a sandbox or two. In Hong Kong and Singapore, regulators are testing the boundaries of regulation for new Fintech and Insurtech companies through a sandbox where new companies are encouraged to play and push the boundaries of regulatory controls. Along similar lines but expanding the sandbox analogy to a much broader landscape, the owners of many Chinese companies are experimenting with CSR and ESG but in their terms and their style. They also have to do this and be mindful of the CG framework they have chosen to follow. In other words, Chinese companies have been leveraging, testing, probing, adjusting, and learning how to attract and kowtow investors from the rules-based SOX regimes of the U.S. to the principles-based regimes in Hong Kong and other parts of the world. It is with this backdrop and beholding the mindset of the owners that the aims of CSR and ESG that readers may need to have before they start reading this book.

Central to the current dialogue in CG is, of course, CSR and ESG … and central to both CSR and ESG is this word "Social." This word bears focus. How should any reader frame their perspective on the concept of environment, social, and governance when fundamentally, the framework underpinning ESG has grown out of a Western set of "Capitalist" ideals? In China, CEOs are not paid hundreds of times more than the frontline workers because such practices would be considered "anti-social" and "not in the workers' interest." A worker's union is mandatory in large Chinese companies, but not so in many Western ones. This practice ensured there would exist a channel for dialogue and to ensure capitalists never exploit laborers. Many state-owned enterprises even have a two-tiered board of directors where workers' representatives are present on the Supervisory Board, and this grew out of the Chinese respect for the Continental European model where large companies are seen as a quasi-partnership between capital and labor, reflective of European "social" democracy. CG with Chinese characteristics meant that co-determination should be respected.

Conversely, many Western companies do not operate in an environment that is considered dirty, unclean, noisy, crowded, or even toxic by any international standard. But many of these companies weren't operating in a world of famine, limited resources, using old technologies and outdated management practices that were prevalent throughout many parts of China during the turn of this century. For one, with coal still being a dominant source of cheap energy, air quality in China is one of the worst in the world and with the world's largest population and high density to boot, environment considerations by any Western standards and any remedial efforts to improve the environment might not work in China. Sorry, wrong medicine. Actions that might be considered impactful in California with some of the most restrictive environmental laws in the U.S. do not carry the same weight for a similar company operating in Guangzhou. Sound your car horns in some quarters in Guangzhou; you might end up in jail. Do the same in California, and they think President Trump is running for office again. The context, history, culture, and practices are hardly comparable.

One may also read this book with a tactician's perspective; focus on the numbers, the scale, and the measurements. Many of us believe in measurement because we realize that to manage anything, we must measure it. Having measured it, a few of us unwillingly fall into the trap, thinking we know how to interpret such measurements because we had been conditioned by our experiences gained elsewhere. The wise practitioners would understand that any measurement is just superficial and meaningless without a proper understanding of the context, history, and practices. (The number five has limited information by itself until one sees that the earlier number was a three and the following number after five is a nine.) Einstein said it best. Everything is relative.

As humans, we search for understanding. We compare and contrast differences and similarities. To be able to solve a problem, one must first understand the problem. Because real understanding precedes any remedial measures, it seems that Lyndsey has started on this journey because she wants us to understand.

Thank you, Lyndsey.

Gregg Li co-authored "Understanding Corporate Governance in China," written with Bob Tricker.

6 March 2021

Preface

I grew up in China, but I have been living in the U.S. for 20 years. While I started my career in the U.S., I have worked exclusively for multinational companies from different countries. In the middle 2010s, I had the chance to work for Chinese multinational companies in mainland China, Hong Kong and the U.S. During this time period, I was often confused by Chinese business practices and struggled to navigate different business interactions as many Westerners do, despite my mixed background. For example, "yes" might only mean "I hear you" and "no" might not be spoken, but should be sensed by the questioner. Additionally, I routinely found myself unable to move forward with projects without being told the true reason. I finally realized that until I understood how Chinese culture influences the way Chinese companies govern their businesses, many of my goals would remain unaccomplished. As a result, I decided to study Chinese companies' corporate governance models and how these governance models influence business practices. This book is a summary of my findings that I hope will help my Western colleagues and others understand Chinese companies more quickly than I was able to. The insights I've gained here will be of particular interest to a variety of groups, including:

- Global investors who are investing in China companies and interested in learning how to evaluate China companies' CG risks
- Corporate chairpersons, board directors and executives from multinational companies with connections in China
- CG, ESG, law, mergers & acquisitions (M&A), management & strategy experts from international consulting firms
- Business school professors and Master-level students in business, law, accounting, auditing, corporate secretary or similar programs

- Scholars or researchers in the field of CG, emerging markets, Chinese multinationals, Chinese economic reform or similar fields
- And anyone who's interested in understanding Chinese companies CG models and China's rapidly evolving ESG movement

While there are a host of books dedicated to China and Chinese business practices, few of them come from the perspective of someone who has studied, worked and lived in both China and the U.S. It's even more rare to find a perspective that respects and admires the good attributes of each culture. You'll find that perspective here which, I hope, will bring greater collaboration and understanding between them.

Introduction

China has been growing fast and in every direction since the beginning of its economic reform in 1978. Since China established itself as the second-largest economy in the world in the past decade, collaboration between Chinese companies and organizations from both advanced and emerging markets countries has been evolving and growing. Understanding Chinese companies' business practices now qualifies as a mandatory skill for board directors and executives from multinational companies.

As China has continuously opened its capital market to attract foreign capital, the number of institutional investors investing in Chinese companies has increased significantly in the past decade. At the same time, some notable Chinese companies, like Alibaba, have enjoyed great success in the global market and positioned themselves as industry leaders. Although Alibaba's innovative CG model has not been widely recognized, its successful IPO at the NYSE in 2014 and its smooth succession plan upon founder Jack Ma's retirement in 2018 have drawn attention to how Chinese companies govern their businesses.

The Western business world often does not realize that China's CG journey only started in the early 2000s, and many Chinese companies are simply going through the same evolutionary process experienced by Western companies decades ago. When Nasdaq-listed Chinese company Luckin Coffee committed financial fraud in early 2020, and Chinese giant FinTech company Ant Group's IPO was suspended by regulators at the end of 2020, investors challenged Chinese companies' governance models and board functions. These apparent failures are indicative of a CG development in its infancy – still learning to walk, occasionally stumbling, but ultimately getting stronger by the day.

Moreover, many Chinese companies have been enjoying the opportunity offered by China's immature regulation environment in the past decades by experimenting, developing and improving their CG system and practices as they rapidly grow into the global market. This approach of "learning by doing" and "correcting from scrutinizing" moves quickly, making it very hard for Western executives and professionals to study Chinese companies' CG systematically.

This book walks us through the history and development of China's CG through case studies. China's CG development has already completed the first stage of learning from Western countries and has moved to a self-development stage with inevitable influences from China's ancient culture and current one-party political system. The book points out major differences between CG practices in China and the U.S. and explains China's CG development path by analyzing China's regulation reforms.

Any serious CG system must address Corporate Social Responsibility (CSR) and Environmental, Social and Governance (ESG), which are currently surging in China. Like most emerging markets countries, these concepts were introduced to China by Western business partners and investors in a different stage of China's economic reform. This book takes us to the origin of CSR in China, explains the important roles CSR played in China's early economic boom in the late 1990s and early 2000s driven by export-oriented business, and how China is reversing its role from CSR follower to leader with self-developed CSR regulatory requirements and evaluation systems. The book then reviews how Chinese companies adopt ESG and are motivated to improve ESG performance driven by widely used global ESG rating systems; it also explains the quickly growing ESG movement in China driven by regulators, non-government organizations and ESG evaluation firms.

As China's government plays an important role in driving regulation reforms, the I also review some ongoing regulation development, like the Corporate Social Credit System (CSCS), the updated ESG reporting guidance and a potential ESG policy in 2021, which will have significant impacts on China's CG development and ESG. I close by noting some promising trends and opportunities for Chinese CG and ESG development in the post-COVID era, recommending that Chinese companies take a leading role in global economic recovery and treat this challenge as an opportunity to establish higher CG standards.

Still, many questions remain. Will China's fast economic recovery from the COVID-19 pandemic make China a model for the rest of the world? Will the upcoming ESG movement in China spur further innovation and development of China's CG? Can Chinese companies enhance their global citizenship because of these phenomena? The answers will be revealed in the next decade. For now, our best predictions will come from a greater understanding of how China's CG arrived at this point in time and how it's developing right before our eyes. Let this book serve as your foundation for understanding.

Part 1 | The Basics: Understanding and Evaluating Good Corporate Governance and Environmental, Social, Governance (ESG)

The term "corporate governance" was coined by Bob Tricker in his landmark book "Corporate Governance" in 1984 (Tricker, 1984). In 1992, the world's first CG report, the "Cadbury Report," defined corporate governance (CG) as "the system by which companies are directed and controlled" (Cadbury, 1992). As an intergovernmental economic organization with member countries representing 63% of the global GDP, the Organization for Economic Co-operation and Development (OECD) introduced the first set of five CG Principles in 1999 to guide policymakers in establishing CG regulations (OECD, 1999):

- The rights of shareholders – requiring CG framework to protect shareholders' rights
- The equitable treatment of shareholders – emphasizing equitable treatment of minority and foreign shareholders
- The role of stakeholders in CG – encouraging cooperation between corporations and stakeholders in governance activities
- Disclosure and transparency – ensuring timely and accurate disclosure of material information
- The responsibilities of the board – Identifying board responsibilities in guiding companies and monitoring management, and board accountability to companies and shareholders

Chapter 1: Ensuring the Basis for an Effective Corporate Governance Framework

In 2005, Global Corporate Governance Forum, an OECD-World Bank initiative, identified four fundamental values of CG (Fairness, Transparency, Accountability, Responsibility) (Global Corporate Governance Forum, 2005). In the same year, the term ESG was first introduced to asset management and financial research in the landmark study "Who Cares Wins" (International Finance Corporation, 2005). ESG has a large scope—Environmental (E) covers "climate change and resource scarcity"; Social (S) covers a company's "labor practices, talent management, product safety and data security"; and Governance (G) covers "board diversity, executive pay and business ethics" (PwC, n.d.). Over time, the performance of the three factors (E, S and G) have been used to measure the sustainability and social impact of a company. And ESG rating systems have been developed and become a widely used tool for investors to estimate ESG risks and opportunities when selecting portfolio companies (MSCI ESG Research, n.d.).

Over the past 20 years, OECD's CG Principles have been updated periodically to reflect changes in the global business world, and CG has developed alongside legal and economic systems in different countries. Moreover, an ESG mindset has become a necessity in the business community. However, the four fundamental values of CG (Fairness, Transparency, Accountability, Responsibility) have never changed.

According to these four CG fundamental values and for the purposes of this chapter, good CG, while developing and achieving business goals and maximizing value, establishes corporate culture and a framework for how a company conducts business, including, but not limited to:

- Implementing and updating processes, procedures and policies according to the principles of transparency and accountability
- Resolving conflicts of interest between different stakeholder groups to reflect fairness
- Managing social and environmental responsibilities

Although ESG covers a broader scope than CG, CG is the core of the entire ESG concept. Good CG is the foundation of corporate culture that drives ESG strategy in a company. Therefore, for the purpose of this chapter, ESG discussion is focused on CG. How then do we measure good CG? And how did governance evaluation systems evolve from CG ratings to ESG ratings?

Chapter 2: The Evolution of CG and ESG Rating Systems in Western Countries

After the Enron scandal and U.S. Sarbanes-Oxley act in 2002, the quality of a company's CG has been considered a key indicator of its long-term performance (Clark, 2005). Institutional investors think long and hard about a company's CG when assessing the risk of their investments and are willing to pay a premium for companies with higher CG. Consequently, demand is high for a reliable, independent CG rating system. The following is a review of rating system evolution from CG ratings to ESG ratings in Western countries, and a list of different rating systems (see Table 10.1.).

- **Quantitative Corporate Governance Rating Systems**

A CG rating is an assessment by a rating firm of an organization's relative position regarding their level of CG competence (Infomerics Ratings, n.d.). Several CG rating systems have been developed by rating agencies, consulting firms and financial institutions since 2002. Among the first rating systems in the U.S., Institutional Shareholder Services (ISS), a privately owned proxy advisory firm, and Governance Metrics International (GMI), a privately owned rating firm, emerged as the most prominent (Sonnenfeld, 2004).

ISS developed three successive CG rating systems (CGQ, GRID and QuickScore) from 2002 to 2015. The latest, QuickScore, released in 2013, analyzes over 200 governance factors in four categories: board structure, shareholder rights and takeover defenses, compensation, audit and risk oversight. GMI formed its Accounting and Governance Risk (AGR) rating system in 2010 by consolidating three rating systems designed by three separate companies. Unlike ISS models, AGR analyzes detailed financial reporting metrics and relies on time-series data to track variable changes over time. AGR scores reflect companies' accounting and governance risk levels.

However, most CG rating systems up to the early 2010s, including QuickScore and AGR, focused on quantitative analysis and were designed to help institutional investors identify investment risks in their portfolios, not to predict future performance of these companies (Larcker & Tayan, 2015). Catastrophic CG failures by companies assigned respectable ISS CG scores have since challenged the reliability of quantitative CG rating systems. The failure of American International Group (AIG), an American multinational finance and insurance corporation, in 2004 is a prime example of one of the most catastrophic downfalls that inspired CG rating system reform. In 2004, ISS assigned AIG a Corporate Governance Quotient (CGQ) index rating of 88.3 and an industry rating of 92 with positive attribution facts like an annual elected board, board-approved CEO succession plan, stock assigned to directors served over one year and a reasonable service fee paid to non-audit accounting and audit service firms. However, in October 2004, AIG was investigated by authorities due to "bid rigging" and using retroactive insurance policies to smooth earnings. In 2008, despite AIG's role in helping trigger the financial crisis, the U.S. government bailed them out (Karnitschnig et al., 2008).

Table 2.1. List of CG rating and ESG rating systems

Company	Rating Systems	Descriptions	CG Rating	ESG Rating	Integrated Rating
ISS	CGQ	Released in 2002. CGQ uses 65 variables in eight categories to measure quality of a public firm's CG. CGQ scores from 0	√		

		(unfavorable) to 100 (favorable).			
ISS	Updated Governance Risk Indicators (GRId)	Released in 2010. GRId replaced CGQ. GRId weights 63 variables and scores from +5 to -5, with zero representing neutral. Positive scores indicate 'low concern" for a company's governance and negative scores indicate "high concern."	√		
ISS	QuickScore	Released in 2013. QuickScore replaced GRId. QuickScore rates companies on 200 governance factors. QuickScore scores from 1 to 10, with 10 representing "high concern" for a company's governance.	√		
ISS	QualityScore	Rebranded in 2016 from QuickScore. In 2016, QualityScore global coverage comprised 6,000 companies in 30 markets. QualityScore scores from 1 to 10, with 10 representing "high governance risk."		√	
GMI	AGR	Released in 2010. AGR takes into account detailed financial reporting metrics to reflect companies' accounting and governance risk levels. AGR uses Very Aggressive, Aggressive, Average	√		

		and Conservative to measure risk levels from high to low.			
MSCI Inc.	MSCI	Rebranded in 2014 from GMI's ESG rating system after MSIC Inc. acquired GMI in the same year. In 2014, MSCI comprised 6,400 companies worldwide. MSCI uses AAA to CCC to measure companies ESG performance from high to low.		√	
Fitch Ratings	ESG Relevance Scores system	Released in 2019, the 1st system establishing correlation between ESG factors and companies credit rating scores. The system scores from 1 to 5, with 5 representing the most relevant ESG factors to credit rating.			√

Source: Author's based on data from Larcker & Tayan, 2015, McRitchie, 2014, ISS ESG, 2020 and https://www.FitchSolutions.com retrieved on December 4, 2020.

- **Current ESG Rating Systems**

An ESG rating system analyzes relevant criteria within each of the E, S, G factors, and determines overall ESG ratings. Different rating providers use different metrics and methods to generate overall ESG scores and rank the various aspects by which the sustainability of companies is assessed (OECD, 2020). ESG rating systems review the materiality of non-financial information relevant to ESG and measure a company's resilience in terms of long-term, industry material ESG risks, and help investors identify ESG risks and opportunities within their portfolio (MSCI, 2020).

The business community's adoption of ESG began in the 2010s. According to the Governance & Accountability Institute, between 2011 to 2019, the number of S&P 500 index companies publishing sustainability reports steadily increased from 20% to 90% (Governance & Accountability Institute, 2020). An increasing number of investors began to recognize the financial relevance of ESG factors on company's purpose, strategy and management quality and make ESG performance an essential part of investment analysis. Rating firms, in turn, were motivated to incorporate ESG factors into CG rating systems to help institutional investors and other stakeholders to measure a company's ESG performance. With the emergence of ESG in global investment strategy and CG rating systems, rating firms either established separate ESG rating systems, or cleverly added ESG indicators to existing CG rating systems and renamed the newer version accordingly to stay competitive. GMI and ISS represent both trends respectively. Therefore, ESG ratings with their integrated factors of E, S and G have gradually replaced the role of CG ratings.

GMI started ESG rating research right after forming AGR in 2010. GMI's 2012 ESG rating system, which incorporated 120 ESG key metrics and 5,500 companies worldwide (GMI Ratings, 2012), rapidly grew to 150 ESG key metrics and 6,400 companies in 2014 (McRitchie, 2014). Also in 2014, GMI was acquired by MSCI Inc. (formerly Morgan Stanley Capital International, a supporting tools and services provider for the global investment community), which simply rebranded the system. With GMI ESG rating's broad coverage of worldwide companies and measurement of key ESG metrics, MSCI quickly strengthened its leading position in the ESG research field and has been widely welcomed by institutional investors. In 2016, two years after an American private equity firm, Vestar Capital, took over ownership from MSCI, ISS

"QuickScore" was rebranded as "QualityScore" and ESG indicators were added. ISS claims its ESG QualityScore is "a data-driven scoring and screening solution designed to help institutional investors monitor portfolio company governance" (ISS ESG, 2020). QualityScore's global coverage comprises around 6,000 companies in 30 markets.

Credit rating firms led by Fitch Ratings are also searching for ways to integrate ESG influence into their credit rating systems. In 2019, Fitch launched its ESG Relevance Scores system, becoming the first credit rating firm to systematically publish opinions regarding the correlation between ESG factors and companies' credit rating scores. The ESG Relevance Scores system emphasizes the importance of governance in global financial institutions' credit ratings (Comtois, 2019). Fitch released its "ESG Relevance Score Framework and Coronavirus" on April 29, 2020 to address the impact of corporate behaviors and customer response due to the coronavirus outbreak, and the potential changes to its ESG framework that could affect companies' credit ratings (Fitch Ratings, 2020).

Today, over 70 firms across the world have developed various ESG rating systems with a three-tiered framework. Some provide fundamental ESG data, some comprehensive ESG scores and some focus on specific ESG issues. However, there's no standard ESG rating system or methodology yet. Investors have to choose the ESG rating system that aligns best with their investment strategy (Li & Polychronopoulos, 2020). Next, we will take a closer look at some MSCI ESG rating systems that are widely used by global investors.

Chapter 3: How MSCI ESG Rating Systems Rate Companies from Developed Markets (DM) Countries and Emerging Markets (EM) Countries

Owned by MSCI Inc., a leading American finance company and global provider of equity, fixed income, hedge fund and stock market indexes, MSCI ESG Indexes' broad international coverage makes it the most popular tool for global institutional investors with international portfolios. MSCI's Global Sustainability Indexes, launched in January 2009, are free float-adjusted market capitalization weighted indexes with high ESG performing companies from two sectors—MSCI World ESG Index and MSCI EM ESG Index. MSCI World Leader ESG Index, launched in October 2007, covers 23 developed markets (DM) countries (MSCI, 2020c). MSCI EM ESG Leader Index, launched in June 2013, covers 27 emerging markets (EM) countries (MSCI, 2020b). The U.S. and China weight heavily in these two sector indexes at 64.2% and 37.89% respectively as of December 31, 2020.

MSCI Global Sustainability Indexes' constituents structure with its sequential selection criteria and quarterly review system is aimed at encouraging companies in both sectors to succeed according to financial and ESG standards (MSCI, 2014). According to MSCI World ESG Index data as of December 31, 2020, U.S. companies' ESG ratings dominate the top 10 list (MSCI, 2020c) (See Table 3.1.), and Chinese companies continue to make steady progress in ESG ratings as reported by the MSCI EM Leader Index (MSCI, 2020b) (See Table 3.2.). While the ESG ratings of top 10 companies in the MSCI World ESG Leader Index have been up and down in the past five years (MSCI, 2020c), the top 10 companies in MSCI EM ESG Leader Index have steadily improved their ESG ratings in the same time frame (MSCI, 2020b). See Appendix 1 for an explanation of MSCI ESG ratings (AAA-CCC).

- **MSCI World ESG Leader Index Table**

Table 3.1. ESG performance trends of top 10 weighted constituents of MSCI World ESG Leader Index

Rank	Issuer	Sector	Country	2020 Index weight	2016 ESG Rating	2017 ESG Rating	2018 ESG Rating	2019 ESG Rating	2020 ESG Rating
1	Microsoft Corporation	Information Technology	US	6.39%	AAA	AAA	AAA	AAA	AAA
2	Alphabet A	Communication Services	US	2.10%	A	A	A	AA	BBB
3	Tesla	Consumer Discretionary	US	2.10%		AAA	AA	A	A
4	Alphabet C	Communication Services	US	2.10%	A	A	A	AA	BBB
5	Johnson & Johnson	Health Care	US	1.66%	BBB	BBB	BBB	BBB	BBB
6	Visa A	Information Technology	US	1.47%	BBB	A	A	A	A
7	Procter & Gamble Co.	Consumer Staples	US	1.38%	AA	AA	AA	AA	A
8	Disney (Walt)	Communication Services	US	1.31%	A	BBB	BBB	BBB	BBB
9	Nvidia	Information Technology	US	1.29%	A	AA	AAA	AAA	AAA
10	Mastercard A	Information Technology	US	1.27%	BBB	BBB	A	A	A

Source: Author's based on data from MSCI, n.d.
Note: MSCI World ESG Leader Index had 721 constituents as of December 31, 2020.

- ## MSCI Emerging Markets (EM) ESG Leader Index Table

Table 3.2. ESG performance trends of top 10 weighted constituents of MSCI EM ESG Leader Index

Rank	Issuer	Sector	Coun try	2020 Index weight	2015 ESG Rating	2016 ESG Rating	2017 ESG Rating	2018 ESG Rating	2019 ESG Rating	2020 ESG Rating
1	Taiwan Semiconductor MFG	Information technology	TW	11.32%	AA	AA	AA	AA	AA	AAA
2	Alibaba Group Holding Limited	Consumer Discretionary	CN	10.74%	B	B	B	BB	BBB	BB
3	Tencent Holdings Limited	Communication Services	CN	10.19%		BB	BBB	BBB	BBB	BBB
4	Meituan B	Consumer Discretionary	CN	3.33%					AA	A
5	Naspers N	Consumer Discretionary	ZA	2.18%	BBB	BB	BBB	BBB	A	A
6	Reliance Industries	Energy	IN	1.89%		B	B	B	BB	BB
7	China Construction Bank Corporation	Financials	CN	1.78%	BB	BB	BB	BB	BBB	A
8	Nio A ADR	Consumer Discretionary	CN	1.52%					A	A
9	Infosys	Information	IN	1.45%		AA	AA	AA	AA	A

		technology								
10	Housing Development Finance Corp	Financials	IN	1.43%	A	A	A	A	A	A

Source: Author's based on data from MSCI, n.d.
Note: MSCI EM ESG Leader Index had 449 constituents as of December 31, 2020.

However, there's no comparing the two indexes. The deviation of industries represented by selected constituents in each sector, especially the avoidance of certain sectors in EM due to ESG quality considerations, and the difference of overall quality of regulation development and economic environment between developed countries and countries with EM, make MSCI World ESG Index and MSCI EM ESG Index impossible to compare at the index level or individual company level. Data shows that in the first three years of MSCI EM ESG Index (2013 – 2016), MSCI EM ESG Index significantly outperformed MSCI World ESG Index, which amplified the impact of selected sector avoidance in EM (Cambridge Associates, 2016). As EM countries increasingly contribute to the global economy (PwC, 2015), demand for one comprehensive ESG index system will likewise grow as companies from EM countries seek an assessment on a unified platform that recognizes their leading position. Establishing a unified global ESG standard will take time, require more research and reform, and require leading companies in EM countries to continuously improve their ESG performance, influence other companies in the EM world and bridge the gap between EM and Western countries. As Table 10.3. demonstrates, leading companies in the EM have started to do just that, with consistent improvement in the past five years and one company making it to the top tier (AAA rating) in 2020. The fact that companies are competing with higher ESG rating scores leads us to ask: What is the relationship between ESG scores and a company's financial performance?

Chapter 4: COVID-19 Impact on ESG

Since the inception of ESG standards, researchers have been studying the theory that companies with high ESG performance are less exposed to systematic risks and more resilient to market crises (Broadstock et al., 2020). The COVID-19 pandemic has provided an opportunity to test the relationship between how corporations have responded to the pandemic and their financial performance in both developed and EM countries. It turns out that corporations leading in ESG have continued to affirm their commitments: Microsoft offered six months of free collaboration software to nonprofit organizations; Home Depot froze prices on high-demand goods; Alibaba Group temporarily waived charging commissions from its merchant sellers. Q1 2020 performance reports of MSCI All Country World Index (ACWI) and Standard & Poor's (S&P) 500 companies reconfirmed the theory that companies with ESG ratings of AAA and AA had average financial losses of 15.6% and 10.8% respectively, while those with ESG ratings of B and CCC had average financial losses of 22.1% and 22.2% respectively (Alliance Bernstein, 2020).

Crises like COVID-19 can change corporate behaviors, create new opportunities, test corporate resilience and amplify the power of good CG in companies' long-term sustainability. Moreover, high ESG-performing companies build trust with their stakeholders because of continuous efforts to care for their employees, partners and communities before and especially during a crisis, rewarding these companies with investors' confidence, partners' support, employees' loyalty and community recognition—and making them strong enough to survive. Continuous research and analysis during COVID-19 will likely provide more data to encourage and accelerate worldwide ESG improvement.

The COVID-19 pandemic may stir a global awakening of sorts regarding corporate purpose. This, in turn, has inspired a wave of stakeholder interest and CSR discussion in EM countries like China, where CG development is rapidly evolving. This creates opportunities for ESG performance improvement and encourages growth in the number of companies adopting ESG standards. According to Ping An's ESG in China report, in 2019, 85% of Chinese Securities Index (CSI) 300 companies released annual ESG reports, growing from 54% in 2013 (Ping An Digital Economic Research Center, 2020). That percentage is certain to grow in 2020 due to significant growth of ESG-themed financial products and total assets under ESG-themed funds in 2020 (Tan, 2020).

Part 2 | The Journey: Reviewing Corporate Governance in China

While CG differs between countries due to different legal environments and economic conditions, some basic elements are common to all. The CG regulation system, including company law, accounting regulations and CG code, defines how a business should register as a legal entity, appoint its directors and relate to shareholders, disclose information and follow filing requirements, and be penalized for failure to obey these regulations. The following is a review of China's CG development in regard to these elements.

Chapter 5: China's Corporate Governance Regulatory Development and Reforms

When Deng Xiaoping, China's leader from 1978–1989, launched China's economic reform in 1978 with minimal regulatory guidance, he called his strategy "crossing the river by feeling the stones." In the past 40 years, China has issued a series of laws and policies to diversify State Owned Enterprises' (SOE) ownership structure, regulate CG and attract global investors. The first set of modern CG code was issued in 2002 and the first revision was issued in 2018. In addition, Shanghai Stock Exchange (SSE), Shenzhen Stock Exchange (SZSE) and Hong Kong Stock Exchange (HKEX) released different versions of the rules and guidance for CSR and ESG report and information disclosure since the late 2000s. Table 5.1. shows China's major CG regulations and ESG reforms since 1978.

- **China's Corporate Governance Regulations and ESG Reforms Timetable**

Table 5.1. China's CG regulations and ESG reforms timetable

Year	China's regulation development and reforms	Purpose of the regulation or reform
1990	Reopening of SSE & Establishment of SZSE	To build foundation for CG development by diversifying SOE shares structure, allowing SOEs to raise funds on stock market, and transferring partial SOE shares to investors
1992	Establishment of The China Securities Regulatory Commission (CSRS)	For CSRS as government body to regulate the new stock market
1994	Establishment of the first set of Company Law	
1999	Establishment of the first set of Security Law	

2001	CSRC publishes guidelines for listed companies on independent directors	To require at least one third of the board members to be independent directors
2002	CSRS issues its first set of Code of CG	To set-up CG code
2002	Introduction of Qualified Foreign Institutional Investors (QFII)	To allow foreign capital to get into China's mainland stock market via institutional investors
2003	Establishment of the State-Owned Assets Supervision and Administration Commission (SASAC)	SASAC as government institution to manage and transfer State assets to the market
2005	CSRC introduces the split-share structure reform and begins converting non-tradable shares of the 1000+ listed SOEs into tradable shares	To diversify SOEs shareholder structure
2006	Establishment of New Company Law and Security Law	To increase liability of directors, improve management structure of listed companies, and make CSR a requirement for companies
2006	SZSE Issues Social Responsibility Instructions to Listed Companies	To define CSR as a mandate for listed companies
2007	New Corporate Bankruptcy Law	To regulate bankruptcy of SOEs, foreign investment entities and domestic companies
2007	Partial adoption of International Financial Reporting Standards (IFRS) and International Standard on Auditing (ISA)	To align China's accounting and auditing standards with international standards
2007	SASAC issues a new directive in Enterprise Risk Management	To provide guidance for state-owned organizations regarding risk management
2008	CSRC requires leading firms to have annual board reviews	To improve CG
2008	SSE releases Notice of Improving Listed Companies' Assumption of Social Responsibilities; SZSE releases Social Responsibility Instruction to Listed Companies	To make CSR required for listed companies
2012	HKEX releases ESG Reporting Guide	To encourage ESG information disclosure
2014	China's State Council issues Planning Outline for the Construction of Social Credit System (2014-2020)	To launch the initiative of China's Corporate Social Credit System (CSCS)
2015	SASAC issues Guidance on Social Responsibility, Guidance on Social Responsibility Reporting, and Guidance on Classifying Social Responsibility Performance	To emphasize the requirements for CSR

2015	HKEX issues consultation paper raising the requirement of ESG reports from "suggested disclosure" to "comply or explain"	To encourage ESG information disclosure or require explanation
2017	State Council mandates majority of external directors to be established in wholly owned SOEs	To improve CG for SOEs and emphasize SOE ERM
2018	Revised Code of CG for Listed Companies (Revised Code)	To improve CG
2018	SSE & SZSE issue ESG Disclosure Guide	To encourage ESG information disclosure
2019	HKEX issues updated ESG guidance with mandatory disclosure requirement	To mandate ESG information disclosure
2020	HKEX issues updated ESG reporting guidance and E-training	To better standardize and improve effectiveness of ESG reporting

Source: Author's based on data from Tricker and Li, 2019, Leng, 2009, State Council, 2014, Wang, 2008, and https://www.hkex.com.hk retrieved on January 11, 2021.

- **Analysis and Trends**

As we can see from Table 5.1 above, there are two phases of China's CG regulation and ESG reform. Phase one (1990 to 2001): In the early 1990s, the reopening of SSE, the founding of the SZSE, and the establishment CSRC as the new stock market regulating authority, launched China's modern CG journey. China established various regulations in phase one to build regulatory foundations for China's CG development. Phase two (2002 – present): in 2002, CSRC issued the first Chinese CG Code, followed by a series of regulations and rules to continuously open the capital market to global investors, diversify SOE share structure, initiate CSCS and CSR guidance and establish a series of ESG reporting guidelines for ESG development (consistent with global trends).

There are a few items in Phase two of China's ESG reform in Table 10.4 worth mentioning:

- The Planning Outline for the Construction of Social Credit System (2014-2020) launched in 2014 initiated a plan for a nationwide CSCS by the end of 2020 (State Council, 2014). Due to the complexity of establishing such a comprehensive social credit system, the process of standardizing the legal foundations of the CSCS and developing social credit system polices and implementation in various cities and provinces is still in progress as of the time of this publication (Schaefer, 2020). Although the completion schedule of a nationwide CSCS in China is unknown, provincial social credit regulations by all provinces are expected by 2023 (Schaefer, 2020). CSCS has received increased attention since 2019 from tension over the trade war between the U.S. and China, especially because of controversial discussions on data security and lack of transparency of the implementation process (Koty, 2019). With increasing concerns about data security as digital business continues growing in China, and greater demand for a nationwide credit system, CSCS development will likely speed up via advanced technology and the possibility of consolidating credit data collected by and held on various organizations. And CSCS will play a significant role in China's future CG development.

- China had been starting to take ESG concerns very seriously with issuing HKEX ESG Reporting Guidance in 2012 and has made consistent updates on ESG disclosure requirements for higher standards since then. The latest HKEX ESG reporting guidance in 2020 has put climate-related disclosure as a higher priority for listed companies in Hong Kong to align with recommendations from the leading international framework for climate-related disclosure, the Task Force on Climate-Related Financial Disclosures (TCFD) (Liu, D., 2020).

Chapter 6: China's Current Corporate Governance Development Status

Like most EM countries, China's CG development started by learning from Western countries, moved into a self-development phase and has become a fluid-learning system. With few restrictions or legal guidance, Chinese companies have created many new, different and often innovative governance models. Leading companies like Alibaba and Huawei (as described below) have demonstrated the advantage of their unique governance models, reaping steady success and slowly gaining recognition from the global business community.

- **Alibaba Partnership's Governance Structure**

With Alibaba's first IPO at the New York Stock Exchange (NYSE) in 2014, institutional investors were concerned about Alibaba's insider controlling governance model that limits investors' influence on business operations. However, when founder Jack Ma announced his retirement, and Daniel Zhang stepped up as chairman in 2018 (see Box 6.1.), Alibaba's succession plan and smooth and successful leadership transfer gained high praise, especially from Western financial media outlets (Laubscher, 2018).

Case Study 6.1. Alibaba Partnership's governance structure

Alibaba designed Alibaba Partnership to ensure the mission, culture and value of Alibaba's business for the long term. Alibaba Partnership is a dynamic group with 35 members as of December 2020. Alibaba Partnership holds one class of shares and controls over half of the candidates for directors. A five-member Partnership Committee within the Partnership is the core controlling group that determines the nomination of directors and future partners and the annual cash bonus pool for all partners.

Alibaba's governance structure has multiple layers of takeover protection: (1) Super-majority provision: any change to Alibaba Partnership's nomination requires 95% voting approval at the shareholders meeting; (2) Proxy voting agreement: Alibaba reached agreements with its biggest strategic partners, Softbank and Yahoo, to ensure that voting power of these two shareholders will not go out of Alibaba's controlling group; (3) Staggered board structure: at each annual shareholders meeting, only one-third of the directors can be replaced.

Alibaba began succession planning almost since its inception (since the early 2000s). Daniel Zhang, Jack Ma's successor, has been with Alibaba since 2007, served as Alibaba Group CEO since 2015 and successfully launched and developed Alibaba's Single Day Shopping event. The company's transfer of leadership from Ma to Zhang in 2018 has ensured continuity of the founder's core values.

Source: Author's based on data from Lin & Mehaffy. 2016, Lucas, 2019 and https://www.alibaba.com retrieved on December 4, 2020.

- **Huawei's Rotating CEO/Chairman System and Superfluid Organizational Structure**

Huawei's governance model is new and creative in a different way, having evolved from a culture with leaders who are unafraid to make bold reforms (See Box 6.2.). According to Tian Tao and Wu Chunbo's authoritative "The Huawei Story," an executive of Motorola China once commented on Huawei's surgical organizational restructuring: "Only Huawei dared to do it, and it had succeeded" (Tian & Wu, 2014).

Case Study 6.2. Huawei's rotating CEO/chairman system and superfluid organizational structure

Huawei's rotating CEO/chairman system was designed to build an effective governance structure to serve Huawei's long-term sustainability. The idea was inspired by the flight pattern of migratory birds, which rotates flock leaders, and by the U.S. presidential term-limit system.

Additionally, Huawei designed a superfluid organizational structure to maximize their customer-centric business strategy. There are two key components of the structure: (1) Rotating middle and senior managers every three years to expose individuals to multiple roles and encourage superfluid culture; (2) Two surgical organizational restructures in Huawei's 30-year history. During a 1996 annual review, all Huawei marketing managers were asked to submit a work plan report and a resignation letter. The company would either approve the work plan report or accept the resignation; In 2007, Huawei went through a resignation and rehiring exercise to optimize its organizational structure—the company asked 7,000 people to resign and rehired 6,581 of them to more suitable positions. Huawei's 2007 restructuring was criticized by both Chinese and foreign media. But its dramatic actions brought a sense of urgency, energized employees and established the tone of Huawei's corporate culture, which promotes dedication, encourages competition and recognizes employee contributions.

Source: Author's based on data from Tian & Wu, 2014.

Despite these success stories, many Chinese companies have overlooked some key elements of CG while chasing growth and expansion. These CG weaknesses eventually became obstacles to their global growth. Specifically, one of the primary challenges for Chinese companies is global branding.

Although there is no research establishing a direct relationship between ESG rating and brand value yet, it's understood that ESG rating does significantly influence brand valuation. Since BrandZ and Brandirectory started ranking the top 100 and 500 most valuable brands in early 2000s, many international brand valuation firms have been navigating brand valuation models and identifying factors that influence the values. Brand Finance's research in 2013 suggested strong correlation between brand value and CSR due to shared factors like market capitalization (Gidwani, 2013). Research shows that companies use CSR as a tool to respond to stakeholders' expectations and build their reputation, in addition to growing revenue and profit in global markets. Top brand valuation firms are employing mixed valuation models with two methods: marketing perception with qualitative analysis which focuses on stakeholders' trust and confidence in the brand; financial perspective with quantitative financial variables which value market share, costs and income. Studies regarding the relationship between brand value and reputation also suggest that a good reputation improves investors' confidence (Alcaide et al., 2019).

The EMI Report on Emerging Markets Multinationals (Casanova & Miroux, 2018 and 2019) shows steady rank improvements for Chinese brands on both BrandZ and

Brandirectory's lists from 2009 to 2018, though some Chinese companies have struggled with brand recognition because they have failed to see CSR as part of global branding efforts. Take Haier as an example:

As the biggest home appliances and consumer electronics manufacturer in the world, and one of the very first Chinese multinational companies, Haier planned to build global branding upon entering the global market in the 1990s and made sizable investments in branding strategy. However, unlike Lenovo and Huawei, who have successfully positioned themselves as price leaders across most product categories and have enjoyed higher brand rankings since the middle 2010s, Haier has struggled moving into the top tier of global brand rankings until the late 2010s (Brand Finance, 2018). And the price of Haier's white goods is still at the lower end when compared with its counterparts in North America, Japan and South Korea, according to 2018 EMI Annual Report data.

- **Haier's Rendanheyi Win-Win Management Model**

Haier designed and refined their Rendanheyi organizational model in about the same amount of time as it took Toyota to create the Lean Manufacturing model, but it has failed to enjoy the same kind of global success (See Box 6.3.). Toyota's Lean Manufacturing model has been widely replicated by manufacturers across the world and has successfully helped worldwide companies enhance their operational efficiency and save costs, establishing Toyota as a global industry leader for decades and contributing to its consecutive No. 1 Global Auto Brands position. Haier's Rendanheyi model did successfully change the company's corporate culture and increase its domestic operation profit. But its limited application slowed Haier's global scaling strategy and prevented Haier from maximizing the business value they expected from the model. And the company's failure to consider the model's legal and social implications held Haier back from being recognized as a good corporate citizen and industry leader in the global market.

Case Study 6.3. Haier's Rendanheyi Win-Win management model

Haier spent 10 years designing, experimenting and implementing the Rendanheyi model, which is labeled as "making everyone a CEO" by dividing the entire organization into autonomous micro-enterprises to motivate service-oriented performance with a goal of "zero distance" to the customer. The model passes business, recruiting and compensation decision-making authority onto micro-enterprise leaders, ties the largest part of an employee's compensation to performance and creates an entrepreneurial corporate culture, significantly improving company net profit for Haier's China operations.

However, Haier's implementation of the Rendanheyi model led to a 25% workforce reduction in 2016. And the compensation model created conflicts between the micro-enterprises' desires for short-term profit and Haier's long-term corporate strategy. As a result, Haier was not able to implement the Rendanheyi model in its acquired subsidiaries, like GE Applications in the U.S. and Sanyo White Goods in Japan, due to U.S. labor law restrictions on mass layoff and Japanese companies' historical stakeholder and societal considerations.

Source: Author's based on data from Frynas et al., 2018 and Monteiro, 2019.

- **Luckin Coffee (Luckin) and Tomorrow Advancing Life Education Group (TAL) Scandals**

China's regulatory flexibility has also allowed opportunities for mismanagement. Most recently, Luckin Coffee (see Box 6.4.) and TAL Education Group's (see box 6.5.) financial frauds in April 2020 have shaken global investors' faith in Chinese companies

---

Case Study 6.4. Luckin Coffee (Luckin) scandal

Luckin opened its first store in January 2018, made its IPO on Nasdaq in May 2019 with 2,370 stores and crashed in April 2020 with 6,500 stores before its financial fraud was revealed. As a typical insider controlling founder firm, the founders group held over 50% of company shares with over 60% voting power and pledged 49% of company shares as loan collateral. The founders' pledge put the business and investors' interests in significant jeopardy. Additionally, both the chairman and CEO held board committee chair positions and compromised the compensation committee's independence and objectivity. Upon admitting sales fraud of USD310 million (42% of 2019 revenue) in April 2020, Luckin's stock price plunged 91%. In May, the company fired its CEO and COO as part of an internal investigation into the sales fraud. In June 2020, the chairman was found instructing employees via email to commit sales fraud and will face criminal charges in China. Consequently, Nasdaq suspended Luckin stock trading on June 29, with delisting procedures to follow. In July 2020, Luckin replaced the entire board of directors with five independent directors with professional backgrounds in the fields of management, corporate finance, law and governance. As of November 2020, Luckin is still traded on Nasdaq with one tenth of its stock price before the fraud. Although Luckin's business continues, it's going to take the company a very long time to repair its reputation.

Source: Author's based on data from Lim, 2020, GlobeNewswire, 2020 and https://www.luckincoffee.com retrieved on December 4, 2020.

and raised serious questions regarding how Chinese companies are governed.

Case Study 6.5. Tomorrow Advancing Life Education Group (TAL) scandal

TAL is a leading after-school comprehensive tutoring service provider in China. TAL has been listed on NYSE since October 2010 and has a small board—only five members, including two executive directors (President and COO) and three independent directors. The former CEO and Chairman, Bangxin Zhang is the founder and controlling shareholder with 29.7% share and 71.8% voting power. The chairperson, Kaifu Zhang, of the Nomination and Corporate Governance Committee is an independent director, who is an assistant professor of marketing with no other practical business experience. TAL's founder controlling structure is no doubt a concern for minority shareholders, and Kaifu Zhang's lack of real business experience as chairperson of the Nomination & Corporate Governance Committee should have raised questions about the board's competency in monitoring management. In April 2020, TAL admitted its inflated 2019 revenue by 3-4% due to an employee's wrongdoing, TAL shares plunged 18% immediately. The employee was taken into custody by local police. TAL did not make any changes to its board structure, and its stock price was recovered later that year due to continued revenue growth with the increasing demand of online education products during the COVID 19 crisis. Despite this recovery, the weaknesses in TAL's board structure raised serious questions as to its long-term stability and security.

Source: Author's based on data from Feng, 2020, and
https://en.100tal.com retrieved on December 19, 2020.

As we can see from a range of Chinese companies, Chinese CG development is still in an experimental stage. Some of these companies—like Alibaba and Huawei—have developed creative CG models and enjoyed great success. Others—like Haier and Luckin— without regulatory compliance and long-term sustainable considerations, have been incapable of meeting their respective growth expectations: Haier has produced a model that faces challenges for scaling up in the global market; And lacking independence and objectivity of nomination committee and compensation committee functions, Luckin's CG model harbors serious and debilitating flaws. While these companies do not fully represent the vast range of Chinese companies, their different stories highlight ongoing innovation in Chinese CG models as they seek to adapt to domestic and international economic and political environments.

While U.S. companies are recognized for having one of the highest standards of CG practices in the world today, that hasn't always been the case. U.S. companies have also evolved as they have explored different CG practices and experienced the obstacles that have come with global growth, the changes in global investors' expectations and regulatory system improvement. Take Google and Oracle as examples:

In 2004, ISS gave Google a low rating in comparison with other S&P 500 index companies due to Google's dual-share class structure and Google CEO Eric Schmidt's involvement in related party transactions (Pender, 2004). In 2012, GMI Ratings labeled Oracle as poorly governed with an ESG grade of F and high accounting and CG risks due to decades of control by Chairman and CEO Larry Ellison, and Ellison's unbelievably high compensation (Fox, 2014). Google and Oracle later improved their CG practices. Google has remained on MSCI World ESG Leader Index's top 10 list for the past five years, and Oracle significantly improved its CG practice and increased its MSCI ESG score.

Chapter 7: Major Differences in Corporate Governance Practice Between U.S. and Chinese Companies

Although U.S. and Chinese companies dominate MSCI World and EM ESG Leader Indexes' top 10 lists, Chinese companies' ESG ratings are behind their U.S. counterparts (see Table 3.1. and Table 3.2.). Besides the fact that Chinese CG development has a much shorter history, there are three major differences in CG practices between the two countries: government influence, the power of SOEs in China and CEO nomination, succession planning and compensation; understanding them is critical to understanding the potential development of CG in China.

- **Government Influence**

Unlike U.S. companies' unitary boards with predominantly independent, outside directors, Chinese companies' CG structure combines elements from both the U.S.' unitary boards and the German-style two-tier board[1] (Tricker & Li, 2019). Chinese-listed companies and SOEs normally have a board of directors with some independent, outside directors, and a board of supervisors with employee and shareholder representatives. The chairperson and most shareholder representatives in the board of supervisors are assigned by SASAC. China's two-tier board is meant to be a

---

[1] The German two-tier board model has a supervisory board with no executive members and an executive board with all executives. The supervisory board sits above the executive board. The German two-tier board requires an equal number of members on the supervisory board to represent shareholders and employees (Tricker, 2019).

structure for Chinese government to delegate its people to the company. With China's flexible CG regulation system, many private companies have created different CG models (as reviewed above). However, all listed China SOEs and most unlisted SOEs maintain a two-tier board structure.

- **The Power of SOEs in China**

According to a 2019 OECD report, U.S. and Chinese companies are positioned at opposite ends of the spectrum of two investor categories when it comes to investor ownership (De La Cruz et al., 2019). On average, institutional investors own 72% shares of U.S. companies, 9% of shares in Chinese companies and 27% as a global average. However, public sector investors (including state and local governments) own 38% of shares in Chinese companies and 3% of shares in U.S. companies, with a 14% global average. Obviously, institutional investors are the driving force in global CG development today, and their light ownership in Chinese companies raises questions regarding Chinese companies' motivation to improve their CG. That said, it's important to understand the progress Chinese companies have made thus far. The diversified ownership structure (including five investor categories—private corporations, public sector, strategic individuals, institutional investors and other free-float) now in place is the fruit of efforts by the Chinese government and other organizations, with China's 40 years of SOE reform starting from 100% state ownership of SOEs, and Chinese stock exchanges' reopening and gradual opening to foreign investors through various initiatives in the past 30 years. Ownership diversification has been the primary focus of SOE reform since its second stage in the 1990s (Leng, 2009). With China's continuous efforts to reform SOEs and open its stock markets to the rest of the world, Chinese ownership structure is likely to gradually appear more diversified and balanced in each category to better facilitate China's next phase of economic growth.

- **CEO Nomination, Succession Planning and Compensation**

In the U.S., a company's board of directors makes decisions regarding the CEO's recruitment, succession planning and compensation. Because U.S. companies tend to tie a significant portion of CEOs compensation to the company's performance, CEOs tend to be highly motivated. According to data from June 2013 to May 2014, 47.4% of compensation packages for CEOs of the top 100 U.S. companies are related to company stock price (Larcker & Tayan, 2015). In China, CEOs and most executives of Chinese SOEs are named by the Chinese government and can be rotated to other SOEs by government authorities, not the board. These SOE executives rank in a hierarchy within the Chinese government system. Moreover, their primary job is not driving up business value, but making sure SOEs remain compliant with the law. Unlike U.S. CEOs' charming compensation packages with stock options, Chinese SOE CEOs' compensation has to align with government officials of the same rank, and stock options are not in the picture. According to 2019 Fortune Global 500 rankings, 23 out of the top 25 Chinese companies are SOEs, which means that a majority of China's top CEOs are not incentivized to maximize company performance. Given that a CEO is not just the head of a company, but its most important leader, the differences in how CEOs are selected and motivated in each country accounts for the many differences in their governance and operation.

Obviously, there are other differences in CG practice between U.S. and Chinese companies, including information transparency and disclosure, decision-making processes, shareholder voting rights, etc. (Liao, 2017). However, these and other differences emerge from the three primary differences noted above. As China's economy continues to grow in the global market, it's reasonable to expect Chinese CG practice to continue to evolve, improve and close the gap with the U.S. and other Western countries. While Chinese SOEs may remain dominant in the Chinese economy, with SOEs increasing in number and share percentage of institutional shareholders, and given SOEs' growing commitment to international regulations concerning climate change and ESG standards, the CG practice and business mindset of SOEs will gradually reflect international standards. As a result, the entire landscape of Chinese CG development will change, facilitating rapid adoption of improved CG practices and ESG performance.

Chapter 8: Comparing Chinese Companies' Corporate Governance Improvement with Regulatory Development

China took a gradualist strategy on economic reform, which has been proved successful when compared to the relatively opposite Russian "rush approach" (Leng, 2009). However, with a gradualist strategy, most of the time countries lack well-functioning regulations, or have out-of-date regulations, which means the development of comprehensive regulations that support the proper functioning of institutions always lags behind (Leng, 2009). CG regulation is no exception.

Nonetheless, regulations and rules are simply the hard factors of CG, like board structure, independent board directors, board committee functions and board report format. CG is much more complicated, subject as it is to the influence of a country's culture, history and legal environment. Soft factors like corporate culture, trust between board members and board directors' knowledge about the company, can't be defined by regulations, but are the result of board members' understanding of the board's functions and fiduciary duties and their commitment to work together to perform these functions. Research shows that these soft factors are actually better indicators of the effectiveness of governance than hard factors. In these soft factors, Chinese companies have the greatest room for growth. Some companies are ahead of the curve, like Lenovo, the Chinese tech giant that built its high standards of governance using Western CG norms as its benchmark. Lenovo has established systematic checks and balances mechanisms in its CG via transparent corporate culture, clear governance structure, a

Case Study 8.1. Lenovo's CG model

Lenovo was founded in 1984 and became a Hong Kong-listed company in 1994. When listed companies in HK were only required to issue financial reports semiannually, Lenovo followed international accounting regulations by issuing quarterly financial reports and began semiannual roadshows to meet institutional investors. Lenovo's 12-member board has one executive director, two non-executive directors and nine independent directors. All members of the Audit Committee and Compensation Committee are non-executive directors. Since 2020, the lead independent director chairs the Nomination and Governance Committee. While Chairman and CEO are still a combined role, the lead independent director calls and chairs meetings with only independent non-executive directors at least once a year. Lenovo's board emphasizes a transparent corporate culture and maintains formal nomination procedures when appointing new board directors. All directors are subject to retirement by rotation every three years, with nine years as regular tenure for independent directors with shareholders elections after the first three-year term. The maximum tenure for independent directors is 12 years with another shareholders reelection. Lenovo's board provides a comprehensive induction and continuing professional development programs to help directors understand business operations and improve directors' professionalism. Lenovo's board keeps a structured schedule, agenda and information dispatch procedure for regular and ad hoc board meetings and annual board evaluation, a clear matrix for key matters that need board approval and consistent timelines for CG reports preparation.

Lenovo demonstrates the best CG among mainland Chinese companies. Since 2012, Lenovo has been consecutively honored with Best Corporate Governance Awards and Best Sustainability and Social Responsibility Awards by the Hong Kong Institute of Certified Public Accountants (HKICPA).

Source: Author's based on data from Lenovo Group Limited, 2019.

professional board of directors, well-structured board functions and a formal nominating process (See Box 8.1.).

As more and more Chinese companies enter the global market, and as some have taken leading roles in particular industries (e.g. Alibaba's Ant Group and Tencent's WeChat Pay leading the mobile payments), the global business community has started to view Chinese companies as global citizens. With this acceptance comes higher expectations of both financial and non-financial performance. This moment presents a unique opportunity for Chinese companies to raise their CG standards to the next level.

Part 3 | The Evaluation: Measuring Corporate Social Responsibility (CSR) and ESG Practice in China

Although China's modern CG development started late compared with most Western countries, China CG development started with integrating CSR in the first CG Code in 2002. This makes Corporate Social Responsibility (CSR) a very important part of China's CG development. And Chinese regulators quickly embraced CSR after the 2002 CG Code motivated CSR evaluation research in the middle 2000s. China's CSR evaluation was the predecessor to China's ESG evaluation.

This section will review how CSR evolved in China and how CSR evaluation systems started, developed and evolved to ESG evaluation systems.

Chapter 9: Chinese CSR and ESG Evaluation Systems

OECD defines CSR as "business's contribution to sustainable development" (OECD, 2001). Milton Friedman, the Nobel Prize-winning American economist, first connected CSR to CG in 1970 (Friedman, 1970) and has been credited for his contributions to the integration of CSR thinking into future CG research (Tricker, 2020). However, CSR was not part of Western CG development considerations until the late 1990s and early 2000s because of increasing societal concerns over environmental and social issues (Tricker, 2020); although for decades, CSR had been used as a powerful tool for developed countries' multinational enterprises when they selected suppliers from developing counties (Gugler, 2008).

As in many other developing countries, CSR had been introduced to Chinese companies by their Western partners as a requirement to meet the Western CSR standard since China started its economic reform in 1978. Compliance with CSR standards was the precondition for conducting business with Western multinational companies. In the late 1990s to the early 2000s, when China's economy grew quickly (driven by exports with mostly labor-intensive manufacturing goods), rapidly embracing CSR became a necessity for both China's government and Chinese companies (Gugler, 2008). China's first Code of CG in 2002 encouraged listed companies to integrate CSR into their business operations (Chen, 2011). In 2006, China's New Company Law provided guidelines for a CSR standards framework and required companies to undertake CSR standards. In the same year, SSE released its "Notice of Improving Listed Companies' Assumption of Social Responsibilities," and SZSE issued "Social

Responsibility Instruction to Listed Companies" and made CSR a requirement for listed companies (Wang, 2008) (see table 10.4. above). These Chinese CSR regulations and standards in the 2000s helped Chinese companies stay competitive in the global market, but they also shifted China's attitude toward CSR engagement from a defensive position of adopting required standards to a proactive position of driving standards development.

Despite these improvements, there were no CG reporting or measuring standards established or required by Chinese regulators at that time, including the 2002 CG Code. In 2005, when China Securities Index Co., Ltd. established the first CSI 300 Index to reflect the performance of the top 300 stocks traded on both SSE and SZSE, the measurements of the index companies were based on stocks' performance mainly by daily average trading value and daily average market value. No CG factors were incorporated into stock market performance measurements.

However, before China had the chance or motivation to explore and develop CG rating systems like the ones in the U.S. by ISS and GMI (as stated in section 10.1.A), the establishment of Socially Responsible Investing (SRI) drove demand for a CSR evaluation system.

- **Early Stages of Chinese CSR Evaluation Systems**

As an investment strategy that considers financial returns as well as social and environmental factors, SRI's origins can trace back to the 18th century in the U.S., and has ramped up in the Western world since 1960s (CFI, n.d.). Today, SRI and ESG investing are both considered as sustainable investments that align both financial and social returns, with ESG investing covering a broader range of E, S and G factors, and SRI focusing more on societal impact (Wealth Management, n.d.).

China's SRI started in 2008 with AEGON-Industrial Social Responsibility Hybrid Securities Investment Fund (SynTao Green Finance & Aegon-Industrial Fund, 2019). Following the first socially responsible fund, the Chinese Federation for Corporate Social Responsibility and the Chinese Corporate Development Academy of Shanghai Jiao Tong University launched the first SRI index in 2009. This marked the official beginning of the demand for CSR reporting and measuring in China. Chinese authorities also introduced subsequent policies and guidance for CSR reports and information disclosure. In accord with the growth of socially responsible investment, Chinese rating firms have developed various CSR rating systems since then.

Runlin (http://www.rksratings.cn) and Hexun (https://m.hexun.com) were the two main rating firms to provide CSR quantitative research scores for Chinese companies in the early 2010s. Runlin's RSK scoring system focused on the quality of CSR information analysis with no horizontal comparison and only covered companies with published CSR reports. Hexun's HX scoring system covered a broader base of public companies and focused on CSR performance analysis with data collected from companies' CSR and annual financial reports. RSK and HX scoring systems established the foundation for future designs of quantitative research. However, RSK and HX's scoring methodologies did not incorporate governance as a factor, and the results from these two systems were hardly synchronized.

Driven by the Chinese government's series of regulations, sustainable investment has grown rapidly in China and made the country the world's largest green bond market in 2016 (SynTao Green Finance & Aegon-Industrial Fund, 2019). The growth of sustainable investment created demand for a rating system with environmental and governance factors. At the same time, with China's ESG reform in the 2010s, research on a comprehensive

ESG rating system began in China in the late 2010s alongside a global trend of ESG ratings replacing CG rating systems (as noted in section 10.1.B); this led to a leap from CSR ratings to ESG rating systems development in China.

- **Current Leading Chinese ESG Evaluation Systems**

Chinese ESG evaluation research started in the middle 2010s following global ESG ratings development. The most local ESG evaluation system in China is "Beautiful China ESG 100 Index," which was launched jointly in August 2019 by the International Institute of Green Finance Institute of the Central University of Finance and Economics (IIGF), a key Chinese research university under direct administration of China's central government authority, and Sina Finance, a media platform providing global financial market coverage and commentary in Chinese. This index comprises the top 100 ESG performers from China's stock markets (35 companies from SSE, 42 companies from SZSE and 23 companies from HKEX). Beautiful China ESG 100 Index's ESG rating system was developed solely by IIGF and considers Chinese characteristics including China's economic development status, industrial distribution, economic and environmental regulation development stages, while incorporating an in-depth understanding of China's markets (since IIGF is directly administrated by China's Central Government authority). In addition to basic ESG factors, Beautiful China ESG 100 Index's ESG rating system added negative and risk elements that take into account violations and lawsuits in regards to E, S and G measurements respectively, and uses A (excellent), B (good), C (qualified) and D (needs improvement) to categorize ESG evaluation results. Beautiful China ESG 100 Index's December 23, 2020 Report reveals the top 10 companies of the Index without publicly disclosing each company's ESG rating scores (see Table 9.1.).

Table 9.1. Top 10 portfolio weighted constituents of Beautiful China ESG 100 Index

Rank	Code	Issuer	2020 Portfolio weight	Sector
1	601318.SH	Ping An Insurance (Group) Co.	17.37%	Finance
2	0941.HK	China Mobile Ltd.	13.73%	Telecommunications
3	000858.SZ	Wuliangye Yibin Co.	9.71%	Consumer Discretionary
4	0960.HK	Longfor Group Holdings Ltd.	4.02%	Real Estate
5	2388.HK	BOC Hong Kong Holdings Ltd.	3.89%	Finance
6	601012.SH	Longi Green Energy Technology Co. Ltd.	3.56%	Information Technology
7	1109.HK	China Resources Land Ltd.	3.40%	Real Estate
8	002594.SZ	BYD Company Ltd.	3.37%	Consumer Discretionary
9	2007.HK	Country Garden Holdings Co. Ltd.	3.35%	Real Estate
10	601688.SH	Huatai Securities Co. Ltd.	1.96%	Finance

Source: Author's based on data from Sina Finance, 2020, retrieved on January 15, 2021.

Another leading Chinese ESG rating firm is SynTao Green Finance (STGF), an independent consulting firm promoting sustainable finance in China. In December 2017, STGF and Caixin Media, a privately owned Chinese media group providing financial and economic news, jointly launched the China ESG50 Index (SGCX ESG50 Index), the first equity index incorporating the ESG performance of listed companies in the mainland Chinese stock market. STGF has been publishing its monthly "Landsea China ESG Development Index Report" since then with regular updates. STGF and Moody started a strategic partnership in October of 2019 with expectation of developing effective ESG methodologies that consider both global ESG standards and Chinese characteristics. After China's COVID-19 pandemic outbreak in early 2020, STGF published "ESG Evaluation for SSE 50 Index Constituent Stocks on Epidemic Control" on February 24, 2020. In this report, STGF developed an ESG Epidemic Control Valuation model (ESG-ECV) with indicators of "S" to assess how companies handle corporate social responsibilities and "G" to measure the timeliness of corporate actions against the pandemic and quality of relevant information disclosure in response to the coronavirus outbreak in China. The ESG-ECV system graded all SSE 50 companies with five performance levels and nine companies are graded at the highest level (SynTao Green Finance, 2020).

The most recent XinHua CN-ESG System launched in December 2020 closely aligns China's ESG evaluation with global ESG evaluation standards. XinHua CN-ESG System was jointly launched by Ping An Insurance (Group) Company, one of the largest financial service companies in the world, and Xinhua News Agency's China Economic Information Service , one of the largest economic information service organizations in China, under guidelines from MSCI ESG Ratings and Dow Jones Sustainability World Index (Liu, N., 2020). Built with cutting-edge technology and comprehensive indicators designed for Chinese companies, XinHua CN-ESG System will provide real-time analysis and ESG scores for companies. With Ping An's leading role in ESG engagement, and its leading position in Beautiful China ESG 100 Index (see Table 10.5.), and China Economic Information Service's State backing and broad range of service, XinHua CN-ESG System is likely to rise quickly and contribute to China's ESG evaluation and reporting standards improvement.

China's self-developing ESG rating systems are still in their infancy. However, Chinese ESG firms' continuous efforts to explore different ESG models and align with global ESG standards are auspicious signs. And just as the disruption caused by COVID-19 pandemic opened opportunities for ingenuity and creativity, these same disruptions may open up unseen possibilities with ESG evaluation development as well.

- **MSCI Corporate Governance in China Report and MSCI China ESG Index**

MSCI's "Corporate Governance in China" report issued in September 2017 summarizes Chinese CG practices through a global investor's lens (MSCI, 2017). The report highlights three fundamental realities of Chinese CG—Variable Interest Entities (VIE) structure[2], State involvement, and controlling ownership. This report points out the legal uncertainty and unequal voting power risk of VIE structure, and reveals the extremely low CG scores that MSCI gave leading Chinese companies that have VIE structures, like Alibaba and JD.com VIE (MSCI, 2017). The report then reviews a large percentage of Chinese SOEs, lists the CG weaknesses of SOEs and details China's incremental SOE reforms. The report also documents the various controlling ownership structures of Chinese companies and corresponding CG risks and concludes that Chinese companies' CG scores cluster around the median of EM peers, and VIEs and SOEs have obvious governance

---

[2] Variable Interest Entity (VIE) structure is a unique business structure in which investors do not have direct ownership but have controlling interest of the entity through special contracts (Greguras, 2020).

risks. In essence, the report laid out a framework for future Chinese ESG evaluation research.

MSCI China ESG Index was launched in March 2018 (information prior to the launch date is back-tested). Around 200 A-share listed companies have been evaluated by MSCI since China A-share officially became part of MSCI EM Index and MSCI Global Index in June 2018. Many overseas-listed Chinese companies have been evaluated by MSCI since 2015. The number of Chinese companies participating in MSCI's evaluation tripled from 152 companies in 2017 to 459 companies in 2018, and the response rate of these companies doubled from 13% in 2017 to 26% in 2018 (MSCI ESG Research LLC, 2019). The overall performance of the MSCI China ESG Index in 2019 improved upon 2018 with fewer bottom-rated companies (20% CCC-rated companies in 2019 vs. 22% in 2018; 36% B-rated companies in 2019 vs. 37% in 2018), an increase in BB-rate companies (26% in 2019 vs. 21% in 2018), and very small changes in other rating categories (MSCI ESG Research LLC, 2019).

The MSCI ESG rating system builds and maintains companies' positions and reputations. Chinese companies participating in MSCI ESG evaluation are working on improving ESG scores because
they understand that global investors welcome higher scores. The ESG rating improvement of top 10 companies in MSCI's China Index demonstrate this trend (MSCI, 2020d) (see Table 9.2.).

Table 9.2. ESG performance trends of top 10 weighted constituents of MSCI China ESG Leader Index (December 31, 2020)

Rank	Issuer	Sector	2020 Portfolio weight	2015 ESG Rating	2016 ESG Rating	2017 ESG Rating	2018 ESG Rating	2019 ESG Rating	2020 ESG Rating
1	Alibaba Group Holding Limited	Consumer Discretionary	28.35%	B	B	B	BB	BBB	BB
2	Tencent Holdings Limited	Communication Services	26.90%		BB	BBB	BBB	BBB	BBB
3	Meituan B	Consumer Discretionary	8.80%					AA	A
4	China Construction Bank Corporation	Financials	4.70%	BB	BB	BB	BB	BBB	A
5	Nio A ADR	Consumer Discretionary	4.02%					A	A
6	Wuxi Biologics	Health Care	2.60%				A	A	A
7	China Merchants Bank Co., LTD.	Financials	1.59%	BBB	BBB	BBB	BBB	BBB	BBB
8	Geely Automobile Hldgs	Consumer Discretionary	1.29%		AA	AA	AA	AA	BBB
9	BYD Co. H	Consumer Discretionary	1.08%		BBB	A	A	A	A
10	China Mengniu Dairy Co	Consumer Staples	1.07%		B	BB	BB	BB	BB

Source: Author's based on data from MSCI, n.d.
Note: MSCI China ESG Leader Index had 140 constituents as of December 31, 2020.

By exposing Chinese companies' ESG performance to the global capital market, MSCI China ESG Index is motivating companies to enhance their ESG and building a foundation for further Chinese ESG rating system development. Although

Chinese companies' ESG ratings are not in the top tier yet, the fact that ESG ratings of most MSCI China Index Top 10 companies have been moving from BB to A and AA classes since 2015 indicates steady improvement of their ESG performance (see Table 9.2.). This improvement also reflects the fact that Chinese lawmakers, financial institutions and Chinese-listed companies understand the importance of an ESG rating and are committed to standardizing and encouraging ESG information disclosure, enhancing regulatory guidance and advocating ESG investment. With China's commitment to become carbon neutral by 2060, China's government has already established plans in its newly created 14th Five Year Plan (starting in 2021) for environmental protection and industrial green transformation. This will facilitate regulatory requirements for Chinese companies' ESG performance and information disclosure (Wong, 2020).

- **ESG Advocacy by Non-Government Organizations in China**

In addition to the Chinese government's ESG regulations and reporting guidance (see Table 5.1.), industrial organizations have been pushing China's ESG reform by leading ESG research, recognition and corporate engagement.

The Asset Management Association of China (AMAC) was established in July 2012 with 147 members in the fund management and distribution industry. As the self-regulatory organization formed to enhance and supervise compliance, fiduciary duties, social responsibilities, sustainability and healthy growth of the fund management industry, AMAC published a "Research Report on ESG Evaluation System of China's Listed Companies" in November 2018 and opened a new chapter in China's ESG investment practice. In May 2020, AMAC published a

"2019 Research Report on ESG Evaluation System of China's Listed Companies" with updates regarding China's ESG evaluation development and challenges.

The China Alliance of Social Value Investment (CASVI) was founded in May 2016 with a mission to develop a quantitative assessment system of social value. Initiated by YouChange China Entrepreneur Foundation, with 60 institutional members and a broad network across many sectors, CASVI is the first licensed international non-profit organization promoting social value investment in China. CASVI published a "Discovering 'SV 99' in China" report in 2017 and 2018 to compare SV 99 (social value of the top 99 companies) and CSI 300 (top 300 stocks on SSE and SZSE) on various social and environmental indicators and economic contribution indicators.

China ESG Leaders Association was founded in August 2019 with 30 founding organizations led by Sina. CESGLA founding firms are publicly traded companies like Ping An, Haier, COSCO Shipping, Bank of Communication and Fosun Pharma. One of the association's goals is to standardize ESG report framework, ESG education, ESG information disclosure and ESG evaluation.

ESG has slowly obtained recognition from different industries in China, as evidenced by the timeline of these organizations' founding and the nature of their different missions. The fact that publicly traded companies have realized the value of ESG and started engaging in ESG improvement in order to stay competitive in the global market indicates that an ESG revolution in China is coming.

Chapter 10: The Context for China's ESG Evaluation System Development

As China's economy grows rapidly, Chinese companies are trying to catch up with their competitors from more economically advanced countries regarding ESG performance and ESG rating scores. In addition, Chinese rating firms and leading ESG firms worldwide continue to optimize mechanical processes like data collection, information disclosure and integration of global ESG and CG standards as they seek a comprehensive ESG evaluation system. At the very same time, it's necessary to consider four unique Chinese factors—legal environment, culture, shareholder structure and government relationship—during this process, as these four factors have had a profound impact on Chinese companies' CG practice. These factors will also play a part in how ESG implementation is integrated into Chinese companies. Though measuring the four factors could be challenging, doing so will make the ESG evaluation system much stronger.

- **China's Legal Environment**

A country's legal environment has a major influence on its CG practice. This is an important factor to consider when evaluating the overall governance level of companies in a particular country. In a country with a weak legal system, companies have to put in extra effort to maintain sound CG and offset the negative impact of the system. Along these lines, the S&P 360 Degree scoring methodology developed in 2004 suggested a "Country Governance Review" as part of the CG scoring framework (Standard & Poor's Governance Services, 2004).

In China, the lack of enforcement of laws and regulations is a weakness which stems in part from the ongoing development of China's legal system and also from a lack of practical details regarding existing regulations. Misinterpretation of regulations and numerous grey areas of enforcement are all too common. Factoring China's legal environment in ESG evaluation can also help identify the weaknesses of the existing legal system and facilitate future regulation development.

- **China's Culture Influence**

Chinese culture inevitably and profoundly influences Chinese companies' CG. Many of these cultural elements contribute to Chinese companies' success to some degree, but some of these elements cause blind spots in their corporate culture and operation.

China's Confucian philosophy, inherent paternalism and relationship-based nominal board culture are good examples of elements which exert dual influences on CG. Ancient Confucian philosophy advocates etiquette and justice, which is helpful when establishing governance rules for an organization, but it also emphasizes compromise and tolerance, which makes it harder to establish checks and balances in an organization, as many employees will refuse to tell the truth simply to stay out of trouble. Paternalism values and maintains long-term relationships with customers and suppliers and rewards and looks after loyal employees, but paternalistic companies are normally controlled by an insider group with opaque decision-making processes. A relationship-based board can be very supportive at a company's early stage by unifying board directors and executive teams, but a nominal board (as opposed to one composed of experts) tends to perform few governance functions and meetings and decisions are simply formalities, which nourishes opportunities for mismanagement or fraud and becomes an obstacle when trying to attract investors. Integrating these cultural elements into ESG evaluation systems requires further research and study on cultural roots and potential solutions. But ESG evaluation systems without these cultural factors will fail to accurately measure Chinese companies' CG.

- **Chinese Companies' Controlling Shareholder Structure**

According to MSCI's Chinese CG report in 2017, 81.9% of Chinese companies have a controlling shareholder structure, including SOEs and founder firms. The percentage was reduced to 79% in MSCI's 2019 research, which shows a trend of Chinese companies' shares opening to global investors at a slow pace. A controlling shareholder structure is not necessarily indicative of poor CG. But from an ESG evaluation standpoint, it's essential to examine whether the board acts in the interests of all shareholders. Alibaba serves as a good example for how a founder-controlling firm engages investors with transparent succession planning as part of its CG practice. On the other hand, Luckin Coffee founders' abuse of the controlling power led to the company's crash and unnerved the market.

Founder-controlled firms also face succession plan obstacles as founders reach retirement age. It's natural in Chinese culture for one generation to pass the business on to the next. However, some founders' children lack the interest or ability to take over the business from their parents. Those willing to take over normally carry on the founder's core values, although younger generations are exposed to Western education and are less emotionally attached to the business. Therefore, whether a company's succession plan is to prioritize long-term business sustainability with the possibility of cultivating outside talent, or to remain a founder-controlled structure by bequeathing the business to the next generation, companies are sure to inherit a very particular set of challenges and opportunities.

More research is necessary to understand the impact of founder firms with a controlling shareholder structure on CG and ESG.

- **Chinese Companies' Relationship with the Chinese Government**

It's one of the most common questions regarding Chinese companies: "Are Chinese companies (non-SOEs) controlled by the Party?" The relationship between the two has been an enduring mystery to many Westerners. Alibaba's Jack Ma characterized the relationship between his company and the government as being in love with the Party, but not marrying them (Leng, 2014). Having strong ties with the government is obviously risky, especially to the extent it allows external influence on board decisions; but a good relationship can also mean companies have access to domestic resources and government support for long-term growth, which ultimately benefits all shareholders. When we emphasize stakeholder interest and CSR from a corporate purpose standpoint, the relationship between Chinese companies and the government might be viewed differently.

Ultimately, it's more fruitful to examine areas where board decisions could be influenced by government, and whether those decisions will help businesses maximize value creation and optimize all stakeholders' interests, than to object to the relationship entirely. Further research on measurement factors and methodologies are needed.

Part 4 | The Future: New Challenges and Opportunities

China's CG improvement has been driven by internal demands to overcome global growth challenges and external requirements from global investors and the business community. ESG evaluation is an inevitable part of this improvement, although there are challenges for China's ESG rating system development due to the complication of the ESG rating system itself, the length of time needed to accumulate and collect proper historical data, the research needed to develop and examine analysis models and many other unique attributes of Chinese CG.

Chinese companies' ESG evaluations are still in a very early stage. Establishing a comprehensive ESG evaluation system requires sophisticated research and experiments. However, with the Chinese government's requirements, non-government organizations' advocacy efforts and Chinese companies' engagement, we should not be surprised by rapid improvements in Chinese companies' ESG rating scores in global ESG rating systems.

The COVID-19 pandemic has raised the importance of ESG with an emphasis on humanity, trust and climate change. Many Chinese companies have shown their commitment and support for ESG during the pandemic by creating positions for people who lost jobs from impacted industries, providing temporarily free services to customers, accelerating vaccine development efforts and aiding other countries in their fight with COVID-19 and the resulting economic crisis. Financial performance data of these companies will prove that companies with better ESG performance are more resilient in a crisis and therefore more prepared to continue to look after their stakeholders and to support the society.

While most of the world has been disrupted by COVID-19, China's effective control on COVID-19 allowed its economy to recover rapidly. Many Chinese companies' steady growth and continuous improvement in financial and ESG performance during and after the pandemic could serve as examples for other EM companies. Although China's one-party political system makes China's CG models unique and difficult to replicate, Chinese companies' CG development and ESG performance improvement will provide valuable data for future studies of other EM countries' CG development models.

With the following actions, China's government has demonstrated that it is aiming to intensify regulation in the coming years to narrow the gap between China's current regulations and ESG standards and global standards:

- The first draft of Personal Information Protection Law was issued in October 2020 to regulate personal information collecting and processing.
- China's initiative of Antitrust law enforcement in December 2020 aimed to target price discrimination and competition exclusivity.
- China is likely to issue an ESG policy in late 2021 with tougher disclosures requirements (Weller, 2021).
- There is a potential for CSCS to speed up its development in order to keep pace with China's intensifying regulation reform.

The government's commitment to higher regulatory standards and ESG standards is expected to motivate Chinese companies to improve their CG practices and ESG performance.

After the 2008 global financial crisis, Chinese companies successfully turned the challenge into an opportunity to refocus their efforts, enter the global market and help position China as the second largest economy in the world (Casanova and Miroux, 2019). This latest economic challenge could be an opportunity for Chinese companies to take a leading role in rescaling the global supply chain system, reshaping China's contribution to global economic recovery, rebalancing Chinese-Western relationships and systematically enhancing China's CG development and ESG performance. If current trends continue, the future is as open as it is unseen.

References

Alcaide, M.A., De La Poza, E., & Guadalajara, N. (2019, March 15). Assessing the Sustainability of High-Value Brands in the IT Sector. *Sustainability*, *11*(6), 1598. <https://www.mdpi.com/2071-1050/11/6/1598/htm>

Alliance Bernstein. (2020, April 16). *Coronavirus Crisis Adds Urgency to Sustainable Investing Agenda.* <https://www.alliancebernstein.com/library/coronavirus-crisis-adds-urgency-to-sustainable-investing-agenda.htm>

Brand Finance. (2018). *Global 500 2018 Ranking*. <https://brandirectory.com/rankings/global/2018/table>

Broadstock, D., Chan, K., Cheng, L.T.W., & Wang, X. (2020, August 13). The role of ESG performance during times of financial crisis: Evidence from COVID-19 in China. *Finance research letters*, 101716. Advance online publication. <https://www.ncbi.nlm.nih.gov/pmc/articles/PMC7425769/#bib0004>

Cadbury, A. (1992). *Report of the Committee on the Financial Aspects of Corporate Governance.* The Committee on the Financial Aspects of Corporate Governance; Gee and Co. Ltd. <https://ecgi.global/sites/default/files//codes/documents/cadbury.pdf>

Cambridge Associates. (2016, November). *The Value of ESG Data: Early Evidence for Emerging Markets Equities.* <https://www.cambridgeassociates.com/insight/the-value-of-esg-data/>

Casanova, L., & Miroux, A. (2018). Emerging Markets Multinationals Report (EMR) 2018. *Emerging Markets Institute, Johnson School of Management, Cornell University*. https://www.johnson.cornell.edu/wp-content/uploads/sites/3/2019/04/EMR2018_V3_FIN-11Jan.pdf>

Casanova, L., & Miroux, A. (2019). Emerging Markets

Multinationals Report (EMR) 2019. *Emerging Markets Institute, Johnson School of Management, Cornell University*.
<https://www.johnson.cornell.edu/wp-content/uploads/sites/3/2019/11/EMR-2019.pdf>

CFI. (n.d.) *Socially Responsible Investments (SRI)*. Retrieved on January 11, 2021 from
<https://corporatefinanceinstitute.com/resources/knowledge/trading-investing/socially-responsible-investment-sri/>

Chen, Y. (2011). Corporate Social Responsibility from the Chinese Perspective. *Indiana International & Comparative Law Review, 21*(3), 419-433.
<https://webcache.googleusercontent.com/search?q=cache:_vmU9pbbFaOJ:https://journals.iupui.edu/index.php/iiclr/article/download/17659/17814/+&cd=12&hl=en&ct=clnk&gl=us&client=safari>

Clark, R.C. (2005, December 5). Corporate Governance Changes in the Wake of the Sarbanes-Oxley Act: A Morality Tale for Policymakers Too. *SSRN Electronic Journal*.
<http://www.law.harvard.edu/programs/olin_center/papers/pdf/Clark_525.pdf>

Comtois, J. (2019, January 7). Fitch launches ESG scoring system to show effect on ratings. *Pensions & Investments*.
<https://www.pionline.com/article/20190107/ONLINE/190109913/fitch-launches-esg-scoring-system-to-show-effect-on-ratings>

De La Cruz, A., Medina, A., & Tang, Y. (2019). *Owners of the World's Listed Companies*. OECD Capital Market Series, Paris.
<https://www.oecd.org/corporate/Owners-of-the-Worlds-Listed-Companies.pdf>

Feng, V. (2020, April 8). Chinese Tutoring Mogul Loses $1.8 Billion After Revealing Fraud. *Bloomberg*.

<https://www.bloomberg.com/news/articles/2020-04-08/chinese-tutoring-mogul-loses-1-8-billion-after-revealing-fraud>

Fitch Ratings. (2020, April 29). *Fitch Ratings' ESG Relevance Score Framework and Coronavirus*. <https://www.fitchratings.com/research/corporate-finance/fitch-ratings-esg-relevance-score-framework-coronavirus-29-04-2020>

Fox, J. (2014, September 19). Oracle: The Worst-Governed, Best-Run Company Around. *Harvard Business Review*. <https://hbr.org/2014/09/oracle-the-worst-governed-best-run-company-around>

Friedman, M. (1970, September 13). The Social Responsibility of Business Is to Increase Its Profits. *The New York Times*. <https://www.nytimes.com/1970/09/13/archives/a-friedman-doctrine-the-social-responsibility-of-business-is-to.html>

Frynas, J.G., Mol, M.J. & Mellahi, K. (2018, July 31). Management Innovation Made in China: Haier's Rendanheyi. *California Management Review, 61*(1), 71-93. <https://journals.sagepub.com/doi/abs/10.1177/0008125618790244?journalCode=cmra>

Gidwani, B. (2013, October). *The Link Between Brand Value and Sustainability*. The Conference Board. <https://brandfinance.com/wp-content/uploads/1/the_link_between_brand_value_and_sustainability.pdf>

Global Corporate Governance Forum. (2005). *Developing Corporate Governance Codes of Best Practice*. The International Bank for Reconstruction and Development/The World Bank. <http://documents1.worldbank.org/curated/zh/194571468330288811/pdf/346690v20Corporate0governance0Rationale.pdf>

GlobeNewswire. (2020, July 13). Luckin Coffee Announces

Changes to Board of Directors and the Appointment of New Chairman. <https://www.globenewswire.com/news-release/2020/07/13/2061507/0/en/Luckin-Coffee-Announces-Changes-to-Board-of-Directors-and-the-Appointment-of-New-Chairman.html>

GMI Ratings. (2012, October). *GMI Analyst Fact Sheet*. <https://d3pcsg2wjq9izr.cloudfront.net/files/47299/download/319535/1.GMIAnalystFactSheet.pdf>

Governance & Accountability Institute. (2020, July 16). *90% of S&P 500 Index Companies Publish Sustainability / Responsibility Reports in 2019*. <https://www.ga-institute.com/research-reports/flash-reports/2020-sp-500-flash-report.html>

Greguras, F. (2020, February 24). *China Variable Interest Entity Structure 2020*. Inventus Law. <https://www.inventuslaw.com/china-variable-interest-entity-structure-2020/>

Gugler, P. & Shi, J.Y.J. (2008, April). Corporate Social Responsibility for Developing Country Multinational Corporates: Lost War in Pertaining Global Competitiveness? *Journal of Business Ethics, 87*, 3-24. <https://www.researchgate.net/publication/226904687_Corporate_Social_Responsibility_for_Developing_Country_Multinational_Corporations_Lost_War_in_Pertaining_Global_Competitiveness>

International Finance Corporation. (2005, October 26). *Who Cares Wins 2005 Conference Report: Investing for Long-Term Value*. <https://www.ifc.org/wps/wcm/connect/9d9bb80d-625d-49d5-baad-8e46a0445b12/WhoCaresWins_2005ConferenceReport.pdf?MOD=AJPERES&CACHEID=ROOTWORKSPACE-9d9bb80d-625d-49d5-baad-8e46a0445b12-jkD172p>

Infomerics Ratings. (n.d.). *Corporate Governance Ratings*.

<https://www.infomerics.com/pdf/Corporate_Governance_brochure.pdf>

ISS ESG. (2020). *Governance QualityScore: Methodology Guide*. Retrieved October 9, 2020, from <https://www.issgovernance.com/file/products/qualityscore-techdoc.pdf>

Karnitschnig, M., Solomon, D., Pleven, L., & Hilsenrath, J.E. (2008, September. 16). U.S. to Take Over AIG in $85 Billion Bailout; Central Banks Inject Cash as Credit Dries Up. *The Wall Street Journal*. <https://www.wsj.com/articles/SB122156561931242905>

Koty, A.C. (2019, November 5). China's Corporate Social Credit System: What Businesses Need to Know. *China Briefing*. <https://www.china-briefing.com/news/chinas-corporate-social-credit-system-how-it-works/>

Larcker, D. & Tayan, B. (2015). *Corporate Governance Matters* (2nd ed.). Pearson FT Press.

Laubscher, H. (2018, September 10). What Jack Ma Taught Us About Good Corporate Governance This Week. *Forbes*. <https://www.forbes.com/sites/hendriklaubscher/2018/09/10/what-jack-ma-taught-us-about-good-corporate-governance-this-week/#3d4a78b49fa2>

Leng, J. (2009). *Corporate Governance and Financial Reform in China's Transition Economy*. Hong Kong University Press.

Leng, S. (2014, October 31). 'Be in Love With Them, but Don't Marry Them': How Jack Ma partnered with local government to make e-commerce giant Alibaba, and Hangzhou, a success. *Foreign Policy*. <https://foreignpolicy.com/2014/10/31/be-in-love-with-them-but-dont-marry-them/>

Lenovo Group Limited. (2019). *2019/20 Annual Report*. <https://investor.lenovo.com/en/cg/pdf/E_CG%20Report_1920.pdf>

Li, F. & Polychronopoulos, A. (2020, January) What a Difference an ESG Ratings Provider Makes! *Research Affiliates*.

<https://www.researchaffiliates.com/en_us/publications/articles/what-a-difference-an-esg-ratings-provider-makes.html>

Liao, T. (2017). Exploring the Significant Differences between Chinese and U.S. Corporations. *Accounting*. <https://scholarsarchive.library.albany.edu/cgi/viewcontent.cgi?article=1019&context=honorscollege_accounting>

Lim, K. (2020, June 5). Luckin Coffee and the Alchemy of Fraud. *High Net Worth*. <https://www.hnworth.com/article/invest/insights/luckin-coffee-and-the-alchemy-of-fraud/>

Lin, Y. & Mehaffy, T. (2016). Open Sesame: The Myth of Alibaba's Extreme Corporate Governance and Control. *Brooklyn Journal of Corporate, Financial & Commercial Law, 10*(2), 438-470. <https://brooklynworks.brooklaw.edu/cgi/viewcontent.cgi?article=1219&context=bjcfcl>

Liu, D. (2020, March 24). *HKEX ESG New Reporting Regimes Effective on July 1, 2020*. Kroll. <https://www.kroll.com/en/insights/publications/apac/hkex-esg-new-reporting-regimes>

Liu, N. (2020, December 8). *Ping An, CEIS Launch China-Specific ESG Rating System*. Seneca ESG. <https://www.senecaesg.com/blog/ping-an-ceis-launch-china-specific-esg-rating-system/>

Lucas, L. (2019, June 24). How Alibaba's Succession Plan Has Paved the Way for Jack Ma's Exit. *Financial Times*. <https://www.ft.com/content/dc6cd806-9403-11e9-b7ea-60e35ef678d2>

McRitchie, J. (2014, July 24). GMI Ratings Offers Webinar on Emerging Market Ratings. *Corporate Governance*. <https://www.corpgov.net/2014/07/gmi-ratings-offers-webinar-emerging-market-ratings/>

Monteiro, F. (2019, January 21). The Multinational Fuelled by Thousands of Entrepreneurs. *INSEAD Knowledge*.

<https://knowledge.insead.edu/entrepreneurship/the-multinational-fuelled-by-thousands-of-entrepreneurs-10821>

MSCI. *ESG Ratings Corporate Search Tool*. Retrieved on January 11, 2020 from
<https://www.msci.com/our-solutions/esg-investing/esg-ratings/esg-ratings-corporate-search-tool>

MSCI. (2014, November). *MSCI Global Sustainability Indexes Methodology*.
<https://www.msci.com/eqb/methodology/meth_docs/MSCI_Global_Sustainability_Indexes_Methodology_November2014.pdf>

MSCI. (2017, September). *Corporate Governance in China*.
<https://www.msci.com/documents/10199/1d443a3d-0437-4af7-aa27-ada3a2655f6d>

MSCI. (2020). *ESG Ratings*.
<https://www.msci.com/esg-ratings>

MSCI. (2020a, April). MSCI ESG Fund Ratings Summary
<https://www.msci.com/documents/1296102/15388113/MSCI+ESG+Fund+Ratings+Exec+Summary+Methodology.pdf/ec622acc-42a7-158f-6a47-ed7aa4503d4f>

MSCI. (2020b, December). *MSCI Emerging Markets ESG Leaders Index (USD)*.
<https://www.msci.com/documents/10199/c341baf6-e515-4015-af5e-c1d864cae53e>

MSCI. (2020c, December). *MSCI World ESG Leaders Index (USD)*.
<https://www.msci.com/documents/10199/db88cb95-3bf3-424c-b776-bfdcca67d460>

MSCI. (2020d, December). *MSCI China ESG Leader Index (USD)*.
<https://www.msci.com/documents/10199/78514cc5-a16d-493a-9774-af1012aa0420>

MSCI ESG Research LLC. (2019, September). *China Through an ESG Lens*.
<https://www.msci.com/documents/10199/e7c3e1a1-d6cb-8b55-1394-ea97fb4fb2df>

MSCI ESG Research LLC. (n.d.). *MSCI ESG Ratings*. Retrieved

January 8, 2021 from
<https://webcache.googleusercontent.com/search?q=cac
he:flsOV3xuYEAJ:https://www.msci.com/documents/1296
102/1636401/msci_esg_ratings_factsheet%2B2017.pdf/61
e32c80-57fe-4fd9-9965-
db951bd559cb+&cd=13&hl=en&ct=clnk&gl=us&client=saf
ari>

OECD. (1999). *OECD Principles of Corporate Governance.*
<https://www.oecd.org/officialdocuments/publicdisplayd
ocumentpdf/?cote=C/MIN(99)6&docLanguage=En>

OECD. (2001, October 8). *Corporate Social Responsibility: Partners
for Progress*. Retrieved January 8, 2021, from
<https://www.oecd.org/cfe/leed/corporatesocialresponsi
bilitypartnersforprogress.htm>

OECD (2020). *Environmental, social and governance (ESG)
investing*. OECD Business and Finance Outlook 2020:
Sustainable and Resilient Finance.
<https://www.oecd-ilibrary.org/sites/e9ed300b
en/index.html?itemId=/content/component/e9ed300b-
en>

Pender, K. (2004, August 24). Google's weak governance rating.
SFGATE.
<https://www.sfgate.com/business/networth/article/Goo
gle-s-weak-governance-rating-2731010.php>

Ping An Digital Economic Research Center. (2020, June 15). *ESG In
China: Current State and Challenges in Disclosures and
Integration*. Ping An.
<http://www.pingan.cn/app_upload/file/official/ESGinChi
na_EN.pdf>

PwC. (n.d.). *ESG: Understanding the issues, the perspectives and
the path forward*.
<https://www.pwc.com/us/en/services/governance-
insights-center/library/esg-environmental-social-
governance-reporting.html>

PwC. (2015, February). *The World in 2050.*

<https://www.pwc.com/gx/en/issues/the-economy/assets/world-in-2050-february-2015.pdf>

Schaefer, K. (2020, November 16). *China's Corporate Social Credit System: Context, Competition, Technology and Geopolitics.* U.S.-China Economic and Security Review Commission. <https://www.uscc.gov/sites/default/files/2020 12/Chinas_Corporate_Social_Credit_System.pdf>

Sina Finance. (2020, December 23). *Country Garden Beautiful China ESG 100 Index Report* [Translated title]. Retrieved on January 15, 2021 from <https://wemp.app/posts/0cbe5690-1797-4944-bdc1-54925509d7a0>

Sonnenfeld, J. (2004). Good governance and the misleading myths of bad metrics. *Academy of Management Executive*, *18*(1), 108-113. <https://pdfs.semanticscholar.org/87f7/96d4c02ab77508c ed40e7f6d26e5db9fe57d.pdf>

Standard & Poor's Governance Services. (2004, January). *Standard & Poor's Corporate Governance Scores and Evaluations: Criteria, Methodology and Definitions*. McGraw-Hill Companies Inc. <https://pdf4pro.com/cdn/standard-amp-poor-s-corporate-governance-scores-2e0f9.pdf>

State Council. (2014, June 14). *Planning Outline for the Construction of a Social Credit System (2014-2020)*. (R. Creemers, Trans.) <https://chinacopyrightandmedia.wordpress.com/2014/0 6/14/planning-outline-for-the-construction-of-a-social-credit-system-2014-2020/>

SynTao Green Finance. (2020, February 24). *ESG Evaluation for SSE 50 Index Constituent Stocks on Epidemic Control*. <https://www.arx.cfa/-/media/regional/arx/post-pdf/2020/03/20/esg-evaluation-for-sse-50-index-constituent-stocks-on-epidemic-control.ashx?la=en&hash=6ED6474F4CC3C2F26683D34AF 86F0BFA24BA796B>

SynTao Green Finance & Aegon-Industrial Fund. (2019). *Decennial Report on the Responsible Investment in China*. <http://www.syntaogf.com/Uploads/files/DECENNIAL%20REPORT%20ON%20THE%20RESPONSIBLE%20INVESTMENT%20IN%20CHINA(2).pdf>

Tan, J. (2020, December 4). *A Green wave of ESG is poised to break over China*. World Economic Forum. <https://www.weforum.org/agenda/2020/12/green-wave-of-esg-investment-is-breaking-in-china/>

Tian, T., & Wu, Chunbo. (2014). *The Huawei Story*. SAGE Publications Pvt. Ltd.

Tricker, B. (1984). *Corporate Governance*. Gower Publishing Company.

Tricker, B. (2019). *Corporate Governance* (4th ed.). Oxford University Press.

Tricker, B. (2020). The Evolution of Corporate Governance. Cambridge University Press.

Tricker, B., & Li, G. (2019). *Understanding Corporate Governance in China*. Hong Kong University Press.

Wang, J. (2008, August 13). An Overview of China's Corporate Law Regime. *SSRN Electronic Journal*. <https://www.researchgate.net/publication/228204574>

Wealth Management. (n.d.) *ESG versus SRI: Successfully aligning your investments and values*. Retrieved on January 11, 2021 from <https://www.rbcwealthmanagement.com/cn/en/research-insights/esg-versus-sri-successfully-aligning-your-investments-and-values/detail/>

Weller, T. (2021, January 7). What's in Store For China In 2021? *China-Britain Business Focus*. <https://focus.cbbc.org/whats-in-store-for-china-in-2021/#.X_eQdS2cbUY>

Wong, D. (2020, November 12). What to Expect in China's 14th Five Year Plan? Decoding the Fifth Plenum Communique. *China Briefing*.

<https://www.china-briefing.com/news/what-to-expect-in-chinas-14th-five-year-plan-decoding-the-fifth-plenum-communique/>

Appendix 1: Acronyms

ACWI All Country World Index
AGR Accounting and Governance Risk
AIG American International Group
AMAC Asset Management Association of China
CASVI China Alliance of Social Value Investment
CG Corporate Governance
CGQ Corporate Governance Quotient
CSCS China's Corporate Social Credit System
CSI China Securities Index
CSR Corporate Social Responsibility
CSRC China Securities Regulatory Commission
DM Developed Markets
EM Emerging Markets
ESG Environmental, Social and Governance
ESG-ECV ESG Epidemic Control Valuation model
GMI Governance Metrics International
GRId Updated Governance Risk Indicators
HKEX Hong Kong Stock Exchange
IFRS International Financial Reporting Standards
IIGF International Institute of Green Finance Institute of the
  Central University of Finance and Economics
ISA International Standard on Auditing
ISS Institutional Shareholder Services
NYSE New York Stock Exchange
OECD Organization for Economic Co-operation and Development
QFII Qualified Foreign Institutional Investor
S&P Standard & Poor's
SASAC State-Owned Assets Supervision and Administration
  Commission
SOE State-Owned Enterprise
SRI Socially Responsible Investing
SSE Shanghai Stock Exchange
STGF SynTao Green Finance

SZSE Shenzhen Stock Exchange
TCFD Task Force on Climate-related Financial Disclosures
VIE Variable Interest Entity

Appendix 2: Explanation of MSCI ESG Ratings

A. What do MSCI ESG ratings (AAA-CCC) mean?

The MSCI ESG Rating (AAA-CCC) assesses the resilience of a company's aggregate positions to long-term ESG risks and opportunities (MSCI, 2020).

ESG Ratings		Explanation
Leader	AAA	The companies show strong and/or improving management of ESG issues. These companies may be more resilient to disruptions arising from ESG-related risks.
	AA	
Average	A	The companies show an average level of management of ESG issues, or a mixture of both above-average and below-average ESG risk management.
	BBB	
	BB	
Laggard	B	The companies show inadequate or worsening management of ESG risks. These companies may be more vulnerable to disruptions arising from ESG-related risks.
	CCC	

Source: Author's based on data from MSCI, 2020a.

B. How do ESG quality scores compare to ESG ratings?

ESG Quality Score (0-10) provides investors with an indication of a company's long-term ESG risks. The table below shows how ESG Quality Scores compare to ESG Ratings.

ESG Quality Score (1-10)	ESG Rating (AAA-CCC)
8.6 – 10	AAA

7.1 – 8.6	AA
5.7 – 7.1	A
4.3 – 5.7	BBB
2.9 – 4.3	BB
1.4 – 2.9	B
0.0 – 1.4	CCC

Source: Author's based on data from MSCI, 2020a.

About the Author

Lyndsey Zhang is an experienced advisor on corporate governance for company boards around the world. She is dedicated to sharing the cultural, historical, legal and economic influences on Chinese companies' corporate governance with the Western business community. She regularly publishes articles regarding Chinese corporate governance and Environmental, Social and Governance (ESG) in the U.K.'s *Governance* and the U.S.' *Global Finance*. Her background as a CFO and VP of Strategy for Chinese companies operating in the U.S., Europe, Hong Kong and other Asian countries, and U.S. companies operating in China, Europe and other Asian countries, has positioned her to understand the challenges and opportunities of both Western and emerging markets.

Lyndsey received her Master of Science in Accountancy from Illinois State University, Master of Business in Administration with a concentration in Finance from New York Institute of Technology and Bachelor of Science in Economics from Xiamen University in China. She also completed Corporate Governance executive education at Harvard University.

Printed in Great Britain
by Amazon

62083079R10061